Whaling for Glory!

Whaling for Glory!

By SHARON SIGMOND SHEBAR
Illustrated by PAUL FRAME

JULIAN MESSNER NEW YORK

Manufactured in the United States of America

Design by Marjorie Zaum

Library of Congress Cataloging in Publication Data

Shebar, Sharon Sigmond.
  Whaling for glory!

  Includes index.
  SUMMARY: Offers a brief history of whaling and
describes the day-to-day activities on board a
typical 19th-century whaling ship.
  1. Whaling—Juvenile literature. [1. Whaling]
I. Frame, Paul, 1913-   II. Title.
SH381.S444   639'.28   78-18247
ISBN 0-671-32917-0

This book is dedicated to my husband Jonathan and to my children, Tom and Susan, whose help and support enabled me to complete WHALING FOR GLORY.

A special thank you to Mr. Frederick P. Schmitt, Curator of the Whaling Museum in Cold Spring Harbor, Long Island, and the many people at the Freeport Memorial Library who helped me locate and obtain the research materials I needed.

Contents

Whaling for Glory!

1 Hussey and the Sperm Whale

ON A CLEAR DAY IN 1712, CAPTAIN CHRISTOPHER HUSSEY AND HIS crew climbed aboard a small boat off Nantucket Island, Massachusetts, and went in search of whales. Hours passed and no whales were seen. Hussey usually kept land in sight, but today he felt adventurous. He sailed far off the coast, and Nantucket Island disappeared over the horizon.

All day the crew searched for the column of white vapor mist that signaled the presence of a right whale. They saw nothing. Annoyed and frustrated, they decided to turn about and sail home.

Suddenly, without warning, a roaring storm swept down from the sky. Strong winds whipped the water, and forty-foot waves tossed the sloop about like a toy boat in the sea. Torrents of blinding spray stung the men's faces and drenched their clothing.

Hussey shouted above the noise of the storm. "Pull them oars. Put your backs to it or we'll never see home again." But it was useless. The storm was against them. A fierce wind rose out of the north and blew the sloop far out to sea.

"Captain, sir," the man in the bow shouted. "Be they serpents or whales?"

Hussey saw several giant forms leap into the air and knew they were not like any whales he had ever seen before. As he watched, one of them disappeared beneath the water. In seconds, its slate gray hump surfaced close to the sloop, then sank again. The whale raised its head and showed its awesome jaws.

"Whale off!" the bow oarsman shouted.

"They must be sperm whales," Captain Hussey said. He had never seen a sperm whale, but he had heard about one that washed up on a Nantucket beach several years earlier. The whale swimming near the sloop looked just like the description of the beached whale. Its head measured a third of its body, and its powerful lower jaw held more than thirty teeth which fit into sockets in the upper jaw, and were five inches long.

"I thought these whales were scarce and couldn't be found," Hussey said, "but there they swim for the taking. Get to your boat."

The surprised men jumped to their feet and scrambled over the side onto the whaleboat. Fighting against the heaving waves, they managed to bring their small craft alongside the whale's monstrous body.

"Stand by your iron," Hussey ordered. The harpooner lifted his long iron rod, then turned toward the whale.

"Give it to him!" Hussey shouted. The harpoon hit its mark, and the stricken whale lurched forward. It gave the men a mighty struggle in the stormy sea, but in the end they won. The dead whale floated on its back. Roaring waves breaking across the bow poured water into the boat faster than the men could bail it out. Their prize would be lost if they could not tow it to shore.

The harpooner gets set to throw his iron.

"Pull to the larboard and draw me close," Hussey ordered.

They rowed to the far side of the whale where the floating carcass protected them from the raging winds. Oil oozing from the whale's wounds spread across the water and calmed the sea around it.

The boat arrived home safely. News of their catch spread throughout the New England whaling towns of Nantucket and New Bedford, and across Long Island Sound to Cold Spring Harbor, New York. Sperm whales were there.

Cold Spring Harbor was, as it is today, a small village tucked into one of the many coves along Long Island's north shore. The Matinecock Indians called the village Wauwe-pex. White settlers changed the name to Cold Spring and later to Cold Spring Harbor.

Records do not tell us when the Indians began whaling. But we know that they waited until a whale swam close to the shore. Rushing to their canoes, they threw spears and arrows until the whale was dead, then towed it back to the beach.

White settlers learned the art of whaling from the Indians, and by 1640, whaling was a thriving business. Whalers cut into small pieces the thick, hard layer of blubber between the skin and the flesh, and heated it in large iron pots. As the blubber melted into oil, black, greasy smoke rose high into the air. The stench spread for miles over the beach, but it smelled sweet to the whalers who sold the oil for money.

In 1705, Major Thomas Jones was granted a licence to

The smoke and smell of the boiling blubber spread for miles over the beach.

"take drift whales" off the southern shore of Long Island. Five years later, he was given the right to all whales found from Gravesend in western Long Island to Fire Island in eastern Long Island.

By the early 1800s, catching whales became a necessary industry. Colonial America had moved toward freedom and independence. As the new nation grew, cities expanded and railroads and factories were built. Whales provided the high-grade oil needed to lubricate the new machinery, to help make soap, varnishes and paints, to process wool into clothing and blankets, and to serve as the chief source of light for homes and streets of the United States and around the world.

Right whales also provided valuable whalebone, a horny substance that grew down from the upper jaw. Colonists carved it into everything from eating utensils to buggy whips. Strips of whalebone held up umbrellas, parasols, and the large hoop skirts worn by women. It was also coiled and used as chair seats, carriage and sofa springs. Some people thought the strips looked nice in the garden and used them in place of wooden fences.

Whale oil and bone were also used for trade. On long voyages, whalers traded them for fresh food and water. In China, they were traded for tea. In India, they bought silk. In Sumatra, they bought pepper. They also bought coffee from Arabia, spices from the East Indies, and hides from Africa.

John H. Jones, the great-grandson of Major Thomas Jones, grew up in Cold Spring Harbor. He watched Nantucket and New Bedford grow into major deep sea whaling ports. By the time he was a man in 1836, over three hundred ships were sailing from New England. Convinced that Cold Spring Harbor should join in the deep sea whaling, he talked friends, relatives, and business people into pooling their money. Together they bought the whaling bark *Monmouth*. A bark is a small three-masted sailing ship.

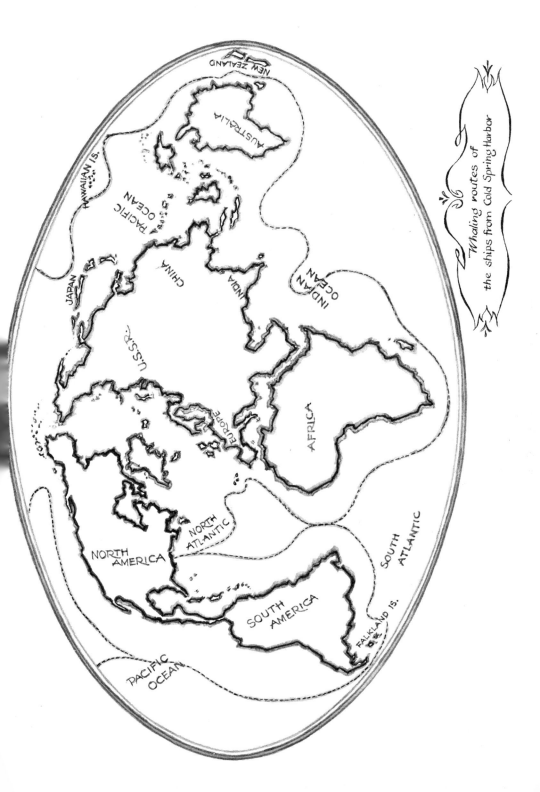

Whaling routes of the ships from Cold Spring Harbor

In the beginning, the *Monmouth* and a second ship, the *Tuscarora*, hunted whales in the South Atlantic Ocean, the Falkland Islands off the southern tip of South America, and near the Azores Island fishing grounds. By 1840, Cold Spring ships sailed around Africa into the Indian Ocean and the Pacific near Australia and New Zealand. By 1843, they had expanded into the North Pacific and spent the short summer whaling off the northwest coast of Alaska. In the off-season, when it was too cold to remain in the Arctic, they sailed to the warmer climates of the Hawaiian Islands, New Zealand or to the Japanese fishing grounds.

2 Signing On and Fitting Out

IN 1854, ADVERTISEMENTS FOR MEN AND BOYS TO SIGN ON whaling ships appeared in newspapers and posters. They promised the thrill of the hunt and the adventure of visiting new and exciting lands. Holding such an advertisement, Peter Dumont walked into John Jones' general store, the headquarters of the Cold Spring Harbor whaling industry.

"Pardon, Mr. Jones," he said. "Says here you need men to go whaling. I guess I'm man enough."

"Are you man enough to pull an oar and to fight a giant a hundred times your size?" Jones asked.

"Yes, sir," said Peter.

"Ever been on a ship?" Jones asked. Peter shook his head.

"Then you're a greenhand. You should know that a

WHALEMEN
WANTED.

Experienced and Green Hands are wanted for the Ship's of the

COLD SPRING WHALING COMPANY

to sail from Cold Spring Harbor, Long Island. Apply immediately to

JOHN H. JONES, *Agent.*

Cold Spring, 6th July, 1839.

---

whaler's life is a hard one. There's lots of work and you may have to eat your pie cold.'' Jones chuckled to himself because he knew the food aboard a whaling ship was terrible, and Peter would not be eating pie until he returned home.

But Peter believed the words he heard. The promise of adventure, and the hope of whale oil money jingling in his pocket drew him and other boys to whaling.

Ships carried between twenty-five and thirty-five men. It was difficult to draw experienced whalemen away from the larger ports to Cold Spring Harbor, and advertisements did not attract enough greenhands for each voyage. Other ways of filling the crews had to be found.

Criminals and boys running away from home were taken on board. Many a drunk woke to find himself on a ship far out at sea. Others, spending the night at local inns, often found their clothes and money missing in the morning. Unable to pay their bills, they were threatened with arrest. A shipping agent would appear and offer to pay the debt and supply new clothes if the man agreed to sign on a ship. Having no choice, the man signed the Whalemen's Shipping Articles. This was an agreement between the company who owned the ship, and the men who agreed to do certain jobs.

Peter asked to sign the articles. The company would pay him a lay of 1/180 at the end of the voyage. A lay was a share in the profits of the ship. Peter's lay meant that he would receive the profits from the sale of one cask of oil out of every 180 casks.

He was to sail on the *Monmouth*. After leaving the general store, he stood for a long time and watched her anchored beyond the sandbar that separated the harbor from the wharf. She was a small ship measuring 100 feet long, 25 feet wide, and 13 feet deep. He knew that from her bluntly curved bow and her square and stubby look she was not meant for speed. Whaling ships had little reason to go fast. They cruised steadily and slowly in their constant search for whales. Her shape made it possible to store in her hold hundreds of casks of oil, food, and other provisions.

Feeding the men was always a problem. Food had to last from three to four years. The following list was taken from a notebook belonging to Henry Edwards who sailed aboard the *Nathaniel P. Tallmadge*. It was supposed to feed thirty men for thirty-two months.

90 bbls.	Salt Beef	800 lbs.	Coffee
120 bbls.	Salt Pork	2 boxes	Tea
50 bbls.	Flour	8 bbls.	Vinegar
4,000 lbs.	Crackers	30 bus.	Corn
1,200 lbs.	Medium Bread	2 tierces	Rice
8 hhds.	Molasses	1,000 lbs.	Pork
7 bbls.	Sugar	4 bbls.	Pickles
2 bbls.	Salt Mackerel		

The days before the voyage were busy ones. Peter could hear the clucking and squealing of animals in crates waiting to be taken on board. He saw the cluttered wharf piled high with ship's rigging, hundreds of wooden casks, and equipment of all kinds. To add to the confusion, provisions from local farms and village shops were constantly arriving. The dock workers could hardly work fast enough to keep up with the constant flow of goods to be loaded on the ship.

Captain Jerimiah Eldredge stood on the *Monmouth* chewing the stem of his pipe and holding a notebook. As each item came on board, he checked it off. When the wooden slop chest was carried on board, he thought of his profit from its contents. The slop chest was the ship's store, and it was kept in his cabin. Whenever a man at sea needed new clothing, a plug of

The wharf was piled high with casks, crates and equipment to be loaded on board the Monmouth.

tobacco, or anything else, he bought it from the Captain who took it from the slop chest. Whalers did not carry much money on board, so the items were charged against them and taken out of their lays at the end of the voyage.

Peter and the other members of the crew returned to the general store for their outfits. Each man received a wooden sea chest filled with a quilt, a blanket, several yards of cloth for mending clothes, needle and thread, two pairs of shoes, a raincoat, several hats, soap and razors, fishing line, eating

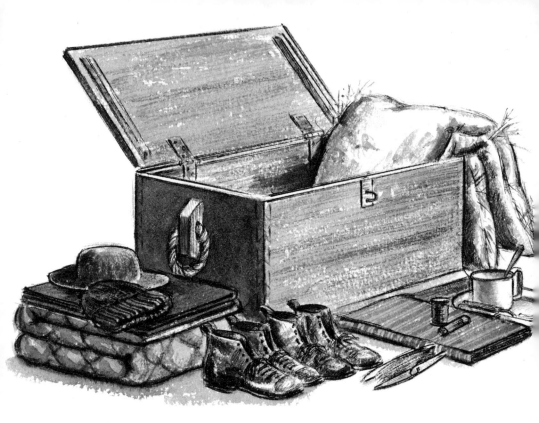

A typical sea chest.

utensils, yarn, a pipe and tobacco, and a mattress. The mattress was called a donkey's breakfast because it was filled with salt hay.

Jones looked squarely at Peter and said, "You get these things now, but you pay for them when you come home. I'll take their cost out of your lay." Peter wondered if he would have any money left at the end of the voyage. So much was being charged to his account. He already felt himself doing battle with some great monster of the deep. Lifting his chest onto his shoulders, he followed the others aboard the *Monmouth*.

The skilled members of the crew, or specialists, went midship to the steerage cabin below the top deck. Harpooners Stephen J. Hardenbrook and Nathaniel Scudder claimed bunks on one side of the cabin. Stilmen Eldredge, who was not related to the Captain, was the cooper. He set up and repaired the casks. Thomas Whitehouse, the cook, Charles Daudall, the steward who cleaned the steerage cabin and served meals to the Captain and officers, and Andrew White, the carpenter, took bunks on the other side. The specialists were not officers, but they ranked above the other crewmen.

Ordinary seamen, or foremast hands, went directly to the bow and lowered themselves through the hatchway into the forecastle (fohk-sul). The small size of this triangular shaped space surprised Peter. The bunks were stacked against the sides with spaces between them so narrow, he would have to be careful getting in and out or he might bump his head or back. There were no chairs, so he sat on his sea chest.

The only light came from a whale oil lamp on a small table in the middle of the cabin. The air smelled of stale oil, pipe smoke, and mildew. There were no windows or ports, and Peter soon realized the only method of getting fresh air and sunlight into the cabin would be to leave the hatchway open.

Peter began to worry as he looked around the forecastle. The ship's timbers were strong and sturdy, but housed hundreds of crawling insects. He wasn't sure he would like living on this ship for two or three years. Some of the other greenhands must have had the same doubts. Several panicked and ran away. The ship's leaving was delayed until some of the boys were replaced, and others were found and dragged back to the ship.

With the crew completed, Captain Eldredge, Chief Officer William Duvall, and Second Mate James Fuller came on board. Captain Eldredge stowed his things in his cabin in the stern. It was a small space, but it had the luxuries of a desk and a sofa. On some ships, the Captain slept in a bed. If the Captain's wife and family were on board, they shared his small cabin. On the *Monmouth*, Captain Eldredge shared his

A cut-away view of a whaling bark of the 1800's.

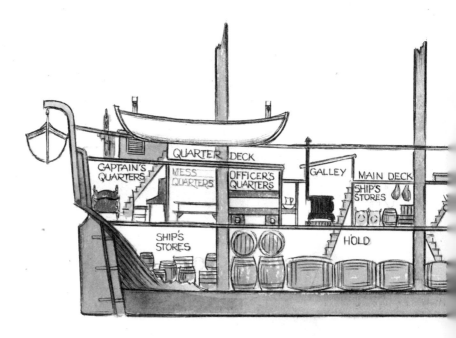

quarters with David Reilly, the cabin boy.

Duvall and Fuller went to their stateroom in front of the Captain's quarters, next to the main cabin which served as the Captain's dining room. They slept in ordinary bunks, and ate in the main cabin with the Captain.

Duvall was second in command. He supervised sailing and the daily operations of the ship. In the *Monmouth's* log book, he kept a daily record of their location, the weather, and the events on the ship. During the hunts, he was in charge of a whaleboat. Sitting in the stern, he manned the steering oar. After the harpooner hooked the whale, he changed places with the harpooner, then lanced and killed the whale. When the hunt was over, he helped direct the cutting of the dead whale

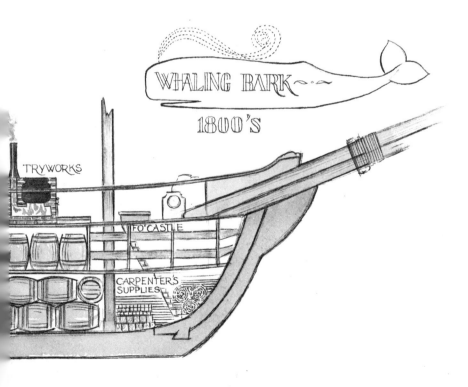

WHALING BARK

1800'S

TRYWORKS

FO'CASTLE

CARPENTER'S
SUPPLIES

as it lay alongside the ship.

Fuller also worked as a boatsteerer on a whaleboat, and was in charge of cutting the blubber into huge strips before it was hauled on board.

On the day they were to sail, John Jones appeared and gave Captain Eldredge his orders. He was now officially in charge of the *Monmouth*. As soon as the tide was right, the *Monmouth* slipped her mooring lines. She was tied behind the steamboat *American Eagle* and was towed safely out of the harbor. When she reached the mouth of Long Island Sound, Captain Eldredge announced it was time for all visitors to leave. Last minute goodbyes were said, and friends and relatives who had come for the ride lowered themselves onto the *American Eagle* and returned to the wharf.

3 The Voyage

NOW THE GRUELING WORK OF SAILING THE SHIP BEGAN. EXPERI-
enced seamen went easily to their jobs, but greenhands found
the work very hard and confusing. They had to learn so much
so fast, and they were unused to the swaying deck. Many of
them grew seasick and ran to the bulwarks (sides of the ship)
to steady themselves, and to throw up.

The crew was divided into two groups, or watches, which
took turns sailing the ship. One watch did the work while the
other watch rested. Two hours later they changed places. Peter
was in the first watch. During his turn on deck, he was sent
from one back-breaking job to another, while others were sent
aloft to begin the whaler's main purpose, to find whales.

The *Monmouth* sailed down the east coast of the United
States. When it crossed the Gulf Stream, Captain Eldredge

Captain Eldredge speaks to his men.

ordered the men to gather below the quarterdeck (a raised deck at the stern of the ship).

"Now boys," he said, "We're going to look for whales, and I want every one of you to obey your officers in everything you are told to do. If you do so, you'll be treated well; if not, take the consequences on yourself and don't blame me!"

The mixture of greenhands, drunks, weathered seamen, and criminals made a crew that was hard to handle. But Captain Eldredge was truly the master of his ship. When he gave an order, quick-fisted Duvall and Fuller were there to insure that it was carried out. Crews on some ships often rebelled against such behavior. Many men deserted in foreign ports, and even whole crews rose in revolt, which at sea is called a *mutiny*. In 1850, Congress passed a law ending the practice of punishing the men by flogging. But four years later, Captain Eldredge could still punish by putting a man in irons and feeding him on bread and water, or sending him into the rigging during a raging storm.

Eldredge stood strong in his position. He was responsible for the ship and everything in it. He was the *Monmouth's* business manager, doctor, navigator, judge and jury. But most of all, he was responsible for finding and catching whales.

After the Captain's speech came the choosing of the whaleboat crews. Greenhands and experienced seamen lined up on deck. Captain Eldredge, Duvall and Fuller walked up and down the line picking the men for their boats. Peter was proud to be included in the Captain's crew.

Day after day, the slow process of changing the clumsy, unorganized men into a working team continued. They had to learn the name and use for every line and piece of equipment on board. They had to memorize the points of the compass and be able to set and break the sails on a moment's notice. The ship's routine was an endless schedule of work, rest, then work again.

Peter thought the ship had been completely fitted out in Cold Spring Harbor, but now he learned that only part of the

The tryworks, showing a cut-away of the interior at the left.

job had been done. Every piece of equipment had to be checked, and hundreds of casks had to be stowed away.

Scudder and Hardenbrook spent hours sharpening their harpoons and lances. Andrew White completed the tryworks, whose brick walls had been built at home. (The tryworks was the big stove on which the whale blubber would be cooked in pots.) Peter helped clean the deck, mend sails, patch his worn clothes, or twisted yard after yard of spunyarn, a line made from old unraveled rope and used to tie bundles of whalebone.

Then came the day that Peter was ordered aloft. Clutching his way up through the rigging, he dared not look down until he reached the topgallant crosstrees (on which the high topgallant sails were strung) one hundred feet above the deck. He climbed into the waist-high double hoops, steadied his feet on the two planks nailed to the masthead, and began to watch for whales.

It was early winter, and the surface of the Atlantic Ocean was very rough and choppy. The waves rose high, rocking the ship forward and backward. Petrified, Peter clung to the hoops and prayed that he would not plunge into the threatening sea below. His two-hour watch passed slowly. Afterward, he was allowed to go below and eat his meal.

In fair weather the crew ate on deck, but in rain or storm they ate below in the forecastle. Their usual meal consisted of salt pork and hardtack and coffee laced with molasses. (Hardtack is a saltless hard biscuit.) Sometimes Whitehouse cooked up a salt beef and hardtack hash called lobscouse. For a real treat, he made plum duff. Stirring together flour and lard, he added dried raisins and apples. Then he rolled the mixture into balls, and boiled them until they were hard. This dessert was served with molasses.

The Captain and officers ate the same food as the crew, except they had fresh meat and butter, until it was all used up.

Captain Eldredge was the first to be served, then Duvall and Fuller. When the Captain was finished, the meal was over. Fuller, who was served after Duvall, had to eat fast or leave the food on his plate untouched.

The men of the *Monmouth* knew they were lucky to have Whitehouse as their cook. Many ships carried cooks who had never seen a stove or a galley. They took the job because they were homeless drunks looking for a place to sleep, or because they were too old or too weak to do any of the other jobs aboard ship. Sometimes boys were too young to be crewmen, so they signed on as cooks. Tom Crosby was a ship's cook at the age of nine. On the New Bedford ship *Condor,* the cook died early in the voyage and a greenhand had to take over. It was a good position. The cook received a lay equal to the whalemen, and he did not have to suffer the danger and hardship of the hunts. He could also feed the men the rotting food and keep the best for himself.

Months passed. The *Monmouth* continued toward the South Atlantic. Only porpoises and dolphins were seen swimming about the ship. They are the smallest members of the whale family, but they were not caught for their oil.

Water on a sailing ship spoiled quickly, and the water on the *Monmouth* was no exception. The fresh food had been eaten long ago, and life was becoming monotonous. Fights broke out among the crew, and some of the men were lashed to

Peter does a two-hour watch in the hoops high above the deck.

the rigging as punishment.

One day the lookout shouted, "Land off!" Peter could see a huge mountain, on Ascension Island, rising high out of the water until its top disappeared into the clouds. They were now near the equator, and midway between Africa and South America. The winds blew warm, and the waves formed great rollers, which broke on the shore with violence. Captain Eldredge ordered the *Monmouth* to sail to the west side of the island, away from the rollers. Then he sent Scudder, Peter and his whaleboat crew ashore to look for food and water.

The landing party rowed into a small bay, and pulled the boat onshore. Where Peter expected to see sand or soil, he found masses of oddly shaped black rocks filled with thousands of tiny air holes and bubbles. They were everywhere, forming high cliffs and deep ravines. Peter broke off a small piece of rock and slipped it into his pocket.

"That's lava rock," Scudder told him. "That mountain you see was once an active volcano. When it erupted, it sent tons of hot lava flowing into the sea. When the lava cooled and dried, it formed this island. There are plenty of islands just like it in the Pacific. Ever hear of Hawaii? That's almost all volcano-built, and the girls there dance and wear skirts made from grass and make a man feel like a king. But we ain't there now, let's get moving."

There weren't many meat-bearing animals on the island, but they managed to capture a wild goat, a few rabbits and some partridges. Later they found hundreds of bird and turtle eggs. Some of the men traveled inland to find fresh water, and others used nets and fishing line to catch fish and turtles off the coast. The men were tired when they finally reached the ship with their last load of provisions, but they knew they would have fresh meat and water—for a few days at least.

Now Captain Eldredge ordered the whaleboats fitted out. Shaped like American Indian canoes, the boats were fragile, lightweight, and could race through the sea as fast as the men could row them.

Each man went directly to his work. Scudder put two harpoons in the crotch, a forked-like piece of wood on each side of the boat in the bow. The bow oarsman covered the heads of several lances with leather hoods, then stowed them in the boat near his seat. Two line tubs were put into the middle, and the tub oarsmen checked to be sure the line was coiled properly. Many a whaler was lost when the line did not run out of the tub correctly, and wrapped around his leg, pulling him overboard.

A bird's-eye view of a whaleboat.

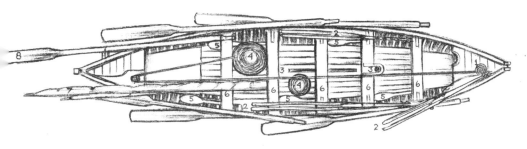

1 Extra line for slack

2 Harpoons

3 Mast seat and centerboard

4 Line tubs

5 Paddles

6 Thwarts

7 Mast and sail

8 Steering oar

When the boats were ready, Captain Eldredge gave the order to lower them into the water. He and Nathaniel Scudder climbed into the first boat. Everyone else removed their shoes to prevent excess noise, and rushed to be the first to get their boats into the water. They had to take off their shoes because these made noise in the bottom of the boats, and the whales, which have very keen hearing, would easily hear the noise and swim away.

Peter helped at the pulleys working the ropes that lowered the boat, then he scrambled over the side and took his place next to the Captain. The stroke oarsman set the rhythmn as the men pulled the long oars.

Whenever the weather was fair, the men took to their boats for long hours of practice. Shouting, swearing, Captain Eldredge tormented and commanded the men until they learned to row as a team. They had to learn fast. It would be too late when a whale was in sight.

It was a calm day when the boats were lowered. But all of a sudden, the bow oarsman shouted, "The warning signal, sir!" Captain Eldredge turned toward the ship and saw warning flags flying in the rigging. "Whitehouse must see bad weather brewing and put up the flags to hail us home," he said. "Pull us back, boys. We'll make the ship before the storm hits." Rowing in perfect rhythm, they reached the *Monmouth* as the sky turned purple, and the sea churned in readiness for the gale.

The weather around the Cape of Good Hope, at the

southern tip of Africa, was uncertain. Squalls, storms, and thunder and lightning showers sprang up without warning, and meant hard work furling and unfurling the sails.

The ship cruised around the southeastern whaling grounds, until it reached St. Augustine Bay on Madagascar Island in the Indian Ocean. Here Peter saw hundreds of strange looking natives speaking a language he could not understand. They came on board, overflowing the deck with exotic flowers and strange tropical fruits. Captain Eldredge decided to remain overnight, and for the first time in months the men were allowed to sleep on land.

Some of the men hated the harsh, strict life aboard the whaling ship and tried to desert. They were caught and held in irons for a few weeks, until the *Monmouth* completed its long and tedious voyage through the calm winds and strong currents of the Mozambique Channel and were cruising father north in the Seychelles Islands fishing grounds.

Although these stops were months apart, and each stop meant fresh fruit and meat, they were also an uncertain danger. If the last ship to stop there had caused trouble, the natives might not be friendly.

Captain Thomas D. Barnes of the New Bedford whaling ship, *Inga*, often traded with natives, and allowed them to come on board without watching out for his crew's safety. In 1851, off Pleasant Island in the South Pacific, natives remembered their ill treatment at the hands of past whalers, and boarded the *Inga*. They killed everyone except two crewmen who jumped overboard and escaped, looted the ship, and set it on fire. When they returned to the island, the two crewmen slipped back on board and took the ship to sea, bound for Australia. But the fire had destroyed the *Inga,* and she could not sail too far. The men drifted without food or water for six weeks until a passing ship rescued them, taking them to Honolulu.

The *Monmouth* spent several months cruising in the Indian Ocean. No whales were seen. Most of the time Captain Eldredge kept the men working to maintain the ship and doing other jobs just to keep busy. To relieve the boredom of the empty sea and the lonely ship, sometimes they caught sharks. Once a shark was slashed with a knife, others turned on the wounded one. Within minutes, the stricken shark would be completely eaten. Or the men would pull the shark on board, stab the hated fish with their knives, and then throw it overboard. Other sharks attacked immediately.

At last, Captain Eldredge gave orders to change the course and head for the Australian coast. The men gave a round of hearty cheers, and set the sails to catch the winds that would take them southeastward.

4 The Whale Hunt

LOOKOUTS TOOK TURNS IN THE HOOPS, SCANNING THE VAST SEA around them. Early one morning, the man in the masthead hoops shouted, "Thar she blows! A-a-a-ah blows!" The men came bursting from the forecastle and headed for the rail to look for the whale. Duvall went below to find the Captain.

"Hallo! Masthead there!" Captain Eldredge shouted when he arrived on deck. "Do you see the whale now?"

"Aye, aye, sir," said the lookout.

"Where away is he and what does he look like?"

"About four points over our larboard bow, sir. (Larboard is the left side of the ship. looking forward from the stern, or back. Today we call this the "port" side.) He's like a sperm whale, making right this way. She breaches! She breaches!"

Peter watched as the whale leaped out of the water, then

crashed back into the sea sending up a wall of water behind it.

"Get below, you in the masthead," ordered the Captain. "Get the boats ready to lower, while I go aloft into the hoops to see what he is."

The whaleboat crews rushed to put all the necessary equipment on board. Cutting, or flensing, spades, paddles, a bailing bucket, the mast and sail, hatchet, knife and lantern keg were all stowed in place. They moved quickly but quietly. Although the whale had poor vision, its sense of hearing was keen. Any loud or sudden noise would cause it to panic and run.

The whale came to the surface to breathe, its blowhole at the top of its head opened. It exhaled. The warm air from its lungs was forced out. As the warm air mixed with the cooler air above the ocean, it changed into tiny droplets of water

A comparison of the size of man, the sperm whale and the whaling bark.

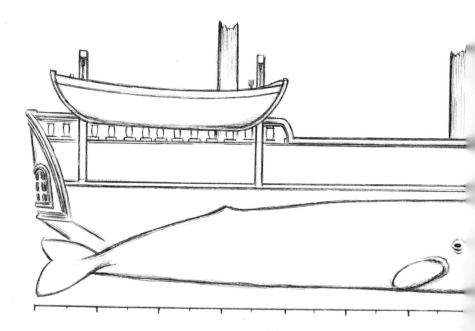

mist. The mist rose high above the whale's head. It lasted only a few seconds, but Captain Eldredge and his crew saw it.

"Thar she blows! A-a-a-ah blows!"

It was a sperm whale. The spout of all other whales shot straight up. This spout rose then angled off to one side. Catching a sperm whale was good luck. Its head contained two substances: oil and spermaceti.

Spermaceti is a waxy substance found in the head case of the whale. The spermaceti would be used to make smokeless candles which were very popular in colonial times.

The whale sounded, dove into the depths looking for its favorite food, giant squid.

"Lower the boats! Lower away!" Captain Eldredge shouted. Within minutes, the men were pulling away in the direction of the whale.

SCALE:
½" = 6' 8"
AVERAGE BARK
90 TO 100 F⁵
SPERM WHALES
UP TO 60 F⁵

"Thar she blows!"

Years of experience had taught Captain Eldredge how far a whale might travel underwater before it spouted again. They rowed near the spot where the whale would surface, then waited

Peter wanted to turn around and see the whale, but he could not do so. The men rowed with their backs to their prey. There were two reasons for this rule. One was to keep up the rhythm of the stroke, and the other was to prevent panic. If a greenhand actually saw the huge body of the whale suddenly rise from the ocean, the size of the beast might terrify him. He might panic, jump overboard and drown.

When the whale appeared, the order was given to pull the oars. The men pulled and *whaled for glory!* This was the whaler's term for racing to see which boat would be the first to reach the whale. Being first was important. It meant possible promotion and prestige at home. The log book recorded how many whales each harpooner and mate captured.

Coming up behind the whale, Captain Eldredge said, "Get your harpoon ready for him. Now, lay to your oars, boys, and pull with all your might and main, as though you were pulling for your lives."

Peter knew they were nearing the whale quickly. As the distance lessened, the Captain became more excited.

"Now boys, pull! Pull! I tell you! Spring hard, and I'll treat you in the next port we come to!"

The men had been working hard, but when they heard the Captain's promise, they pulled their oars even harder. The whaleboat raced on with lightning speed.

"Captain, can I dart now? I'm near enough!" cried Nat Scudder.

"I'll tell you when you're near enough!" Captain Eldredge said. "Pull away! Why don't you pull boys! There he is, only a ship's length off. Heave up your oars and take to your paddles. Easy now, and quiet. Stand up Nat and grab your iron. Look for him, he's right ahead!"

Nat stopped rowing. He stood up, placed his knee in the cleat for balance, then lifted the heavy harpoon and faced the giant whale.

"I see him," he said. "Lay me close as possible."

Within seconds, the boat was in the correct position.

"Give it to him!" Captain Eldredge shouted.

With all his strength, Nat drove the first harpoon deep into the whale's blubber. Then he threw the second harpoon. The harpoons did not kill the whale. They hooked it so that it could not escape. The stricken whale leaped with pain.

"Change places!" Captain Eldredge commanded. Nat now turned away from the whale and started to make his way to the stern. At the same time, the Captain was climbing over Peter and the equipment until he took Nat's place in the bow. Captain Eldredge would be the one to lance and finally kill the

The thrashing whale breaches.

whale. Nat, now in the stern, became the boatsteerer. This changing of places was dangerous as the whale thrashed about sweeping the sea into huge, violent waves. The oarsmen tried to prevent the boat from capsizing while the two men changed positions.

Suddenly the full length of the whale's body rose into the air above the boat.

"She breaches! Stern all!" exclaimed the Captain. The men rowed back, away from the thundering blows of the thrashing flukes.

The whale dove, then leaped again, churning the sea into a fury of splashing white water. Suddenly it darted forward at

an amazing speed, dragging the boat behind it in a "Nantucket Sleigh Ride."

As the whale continued to rush forward, more and more of the rope ran out of the line tubs. Captain Eldredge wrapped the line around the loggerhead, a thick piece of timber in the stern. The rope smoked, and the tub oarsman soaked it with sea water to prevent friction from setting it afire. The line grew tight and stiff, as the boat was pulled by the whale.

For several hours the whale dashed wildly through miles of water. Flying spray tore at the men's faces. They gripped the sides of the boat as the whale dove and leaped over and over again in an attempt to free itself from the harpoons.

At last it began to weaken. Its pace slowed as its energy drained. Finally, unable to swim on, the whale stopped and tried to regain its strength.

The bow oarsman picked up the lances and removed their covers. He placed them in the crotch where Captain Eldredge could reach them.

"Lay me close," Captain Eldredge said. "But, before the men could obey his command, the whale darted forward, then turned and rushed straight toward the boat. It lifted its head as it swam. It looked as though it were trying to crush the men to death with its angry rage. Quickly the men changed direction and the whale missed its mark. But in an instant, it leaped and threw itself across the bow. Captain Eldredge, already on his feet, drove the lance deep into its body.

The whale slid off the boat and sank beneath the water.

The men waited with pounding hearts, watching the water in silence. Peter noticed that Duvall's boat had caught up to them and was waiting, ready to attack at any moment.

They were not kept waiting long. The whale returned to the surface spouting blood, spraying it everywhere. It soaked the men, the boats, and the sea around it.

Captain Eldredge ordered Duvall to throw another harpoon. In seconds the mate's boat raced forward and another harpoon sank deep into the whale's flesh. It dove, writhing with pain. "Now stand to your oars, boys, and be ready to pull stoutly," Captain Eldredge told them. "We'll see some stirring sport when he returns, or I'm mistaken."

The huge flukes rose high into the air, then came crashing down again and again trying to smash its enemies and pull them into the sea. Every time the flukes rose, they threw giant sheets of water that filled the Captain's boat.

"Now's your time, Mr. Duvall," Captain Eldredge shouted to the Chief Officer. "Haul upon him and give him a good dance."

In seconds, Duvall's boat lay alongside the huge body, with the bow touching its back. Duvall punched his lance up and down, making dozens of holes in the whale's side. "Stern me off" he cried.

The whale began to move again. "Spring men. Spring for your lives," the Captain shouted. "He's coming up for a fight." In the next moment, the whale came up and with a burst of energy, thrashed about, whipping the waves into

As the men jumped overboard, the whale crushed the boat to splinters.

whirlpools of bloody foam.

By now the Captain's boat was entirely filled with water and could not row away. "He's coming for us, boys. Take to the sea," Captain Eldredge shouted as the whale rushed straight toward the helpless boat.

Everyone jumped into the water. Just as the last man left the boat, the whale came rushing at it head-on with its awesome mouth wide open. Its massive jaws bit down hard and crushed the boat to splinters. Then, exhausted, it slid beneath the surface to rest.

For the next thirty minutes, the water lay calm, red with blood. The crew treaded water to stay afloat.

The whale surfaced once more. With a last burst of energy, it swam around and around in smaller and smaller circles. Again it beat the water with its flukes. Then its death flurry ended. The whale rolled over onto one side, threw its fin up, and sank back dead.

Exhausted and dripping, the men gave three cheers and were pulled into the mate's boat. The crushed and splintered boat was collected to be saved for firewood. To signal the ship that the whale was dead, a piece of black cloth was tied to a pole and stuck into its back.

Most of the greenhands had been both excited and terrified by their experience, and many of them vowed to run away rather than face another monster of the deep. Peter watched the whale which looked like a motionless island in the sea, and realized that his first whale hunt had ended.

5 Cutting In

THE *MONMOUTH* SAILED TO MEET THE WHALEBOAT, AND BY NOON the whale was alongside. A platform, or cutting stage, made of three wooden planks with an iron railing in front, was lowered over the whale. The three men who would do the butchering tied heavy ropes around their waists to keep from falling into the water and walked onto the platform.

As soon as the first cut was made in the whale's side, streams of blood gushed out. Within seconds, the water was filled with hungry sharks. The men worked fast so they would not lose great chunks to the sharks.

Slits were cut in the blubber just behind the eyes.

The men on the cutting stage begin to butcher the whale. ▶

Nathaniel Scudder stood on the whale and pushed the blubber hook through the slits. Then slits were cut all along the whale's body to the flukes.

"Haul away," shouted Duvall. The men pulled the ropes working the blocks and tackles to raise the blubber hook. Men on the cutting stage hacked away at the blubber with long flensing spades. As they worked, a large strip of blubber called the blanket piece was ripped away from the body and swung over the deck. Suddenly the ship listed toward the whale almost throwing Peter off his feet.

"Way 'nough," Duvall shouted. The men stopped pulling at the ropes. Another hole was hacked into the blubber, and a second hook was attached. Using sharp tools, the blubber was sliced in half, and both pieces slid through the hatch into the blubber room below.

"Heave away," Duvall said. The hooks were attached to the whale's side again. As the blubber was being stripped away, the body revolved slowly, unwinding like the skin of an apple being cut in a single peel.

Wood and carpenter's shavings were fed into the fire that had been started in the tryworks. A tank beneath held water and prevented the planks and deck from catching on fire. There was a roof over the trypots to protect the bubbling oil from rain.

Thick, black smoke rose from the pots as the blubber cooked. It blackened the deck, the sails and the men.

Peter was sent to work in the room below. He had to

grasp the arm of the man next to him to prevent himself from falling into the thick, slimy blubber. He also had to keep out of the way of new blubber strips falling through the hatch. When Peter was able to keep his balance, he helped cut the blubber into small pieces, then into thin slices called "Bible leaves" to try to get more oil out of them. One at a time, they were fed into the 250-gallon pots.

When the pieces were tried out, they shriveled and floated to the top. (Trying out means getting the whale oil out of the blubber by boiling.) Now the blubber pieces were called scraps. The scraps were skimmed off and thrown into the fire as fuel. Some of the men liked to eat the scraps. They tasted like pork cracklings, or strips of fried pork skin.

While the oil was cooking, Whitehouse dropped sweet dough into the pots and made doughnut puffs. This was a welcome addition to the usual meal.

Captain Eldredge stood on the cutting stage and tied a rope around his waist. He reached inside the whale's intestines looking for valuable ambergris. He was sure he would find nothing as this looked like a healthy whale, and ambergris formed only in the intestines of sick sperm whales. Still, he had to be sure.

Ambergris looked like huge rubber sponges and was usually found in chucks of 200 pounds and more. It was used in religious rites in some churches, and as a flavoring for food by the Indians. Its most popular use was as a fixative for perfume. Ambergris absorbed the scent and held it for long periods of time. This meant that perfume could last several months.

Finding ambergris meant riches for the investors, the captain and the crew. It sold for $200 to $400 a pound, and could mean a profit of over $80,000. But Captain Eldredge found nothing.

Two holes were cut into the whale's head. A chain was pushed through the holes, and the head was taken on board. The jaw was cut apart, and the lower portion stored on the foredeck. It was left to rot so the teeth and bones could be taken out and used for scrimshaw, the whaler's art. Scrimshaw is carving or engraving on whalebone, ivory, teeth or shells.

The upper part of the head was opened. Two men took their shirts off, then climbed inside. They used wooden buckets to bail out the hot, greasy, clear white oil. It had a sweet scent. The oil and spermaceti were heated to keep them from spoiling, then stored in casks.

Several men scraped out the white spongy stuff that grew in the upper jaw. This was dumped into pots and boiled. The rest of the head was cut up and boiled, too.

It took two hours to cook all the oil out of one pot of blubber. Then it was put into cooling tanks, and later transferred to permanent casks and stored below. What was left of the whale was cut free and left for the sharks.

While the cutting continued, the rest of the crew took turns working six hours on deck, then sleeping six hours. The sun went down and the light grew dim. Soon all that could be seen were the stars and the glowing flames from the tryworks.

Another day passed, and at last the trying out was finished. The whale had been a big one. It gave 100 barrels of oil.

Now the work of cleaning the ship began. The crew stood knee deep in gurry, a mixture of blood, slime and grease. The gurry was everywhere. It seeped into the Captain's cabin and into the galley where the food was cooked: It seeped into the hold and into the forecastle where the crew slept.

The crew spent the next three days scrubbing the sails, and washing and polishing the deck until the ship was sparkling clean. But they could not rid the *Monmouth* of the sickening smell of oil turning rancid in the casks.

6 Scrimshaw and a Gam

HOPING TO SIGHT ANOTHER WHALE, CAPTAIN ELDREDGE ORDERED the *Monmouth* to continue cruising off the Australian coast. At first, talking about the whale they had caught kept the men's spirits high. But after a time, the talk died down and the daily routine became tiresome.

A whaler's clothes had to be washed every two days. His blanket had to be washed every week, and his mattress had to be emptied so that the ticking could be cleaned. The straw was shaken every other day to prevent it from matting and molding. Washing the clothes was not hard. But Peter found it difficult to wash the bulky blanket on the scrub boards.

David Reilly, the cabin boy, could often be seen scrubbing the stairway to the quarterdeck, or helping Whitehouse break out barrels of food. Sometimes they threw food overboard because it was rotten or wormy.

Peter learns how to build new casks from the cooper.

Peter often helped the cooper, Stilman Eldredge, splash water over the casks filled with oil. The water soaked into the wooden slats causing them to swell until they pushed together so tightly that the casks became leakproof. Peter also learned how to build new casks to store the oil from the next whale hunt.

During the evening dog watches (the sailors' name for a late evening watch), the light was too dim to search for whales. All hands came on deck or sat in the forecastle relaxing, smoking, mending their clothes, singing the old whaler's songs, and telling stories of daring sea voyages and near escapes from flesh-eating natives on tropical islands.

One of Peter's favorite stories was of the ship *Splendid* sailing out of Cold Spring Harbor and Captain Pierson. The *Splendid* is believed to have been the second whaling ship to legally enter Japan. While off the northern islands, Captain Pierson sighted an abandoned Japanese junk. Taking the small boat in tow, he sailed into the nearest Japanese port. Several officials came on board and took every man to a beautiful park, where they bathed in the cool, clear pools and dressed in oriental robes. From there they went to a large hall where they were served course after course of delicious oriental foods and delicate drinks. After the meal, the men returned to the pools, bathed again, and were ordered to go to sea. They were warned that if they ever entered another Japanese port, every man would be beheaded.

Several weeks passed, and the jawbone laying on the foredeck of the *Monmouth* had rotted in the sun. At last, it was ready for scrimshaw. The teeth and some of the bone were soaked in a tub of salt brine. When they were ready, they were removed from the tub, rubbed smooth with a piece of shark skin, and polished with ashes from the tryworks fire.

Finally, the men began scratching in a design with their jack knives. Some men copied pictures they found in magazines and newspapers they had brought with them.

Others used pictures of their sweethearts or wives. At last, the design was complete. But it was hard to see. Using their thumb and palm, the whalers rubbed black ink into the scratches until the picture stood out clearly. It took a long time to finish a piece of scrimshaw. One man is known to have worked six months on a single tooth.

Most scrimshaw work was given as gifts to friends and relatives. Some of the men of the *Monmouth* carved decorated jagging wheels used to seal pie dough. Among the most popular scrimshaw pieces were rolling pins, work boxes, canes, clothespins, toys and games. The most skillful artists used the smallest pieces of teeth and bone to make jewelry and buttons.

Some of the scrimshaw carved by whalers.

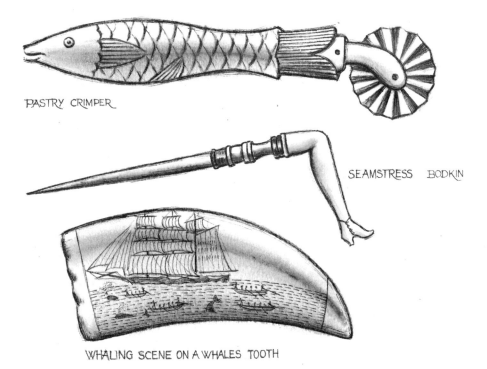

PASTRY CRIMPER

SEAMSTRESS BODKIN

WHALING SCENE ON A WHALES TOOTH

Longer pieces of bone were finished into yarn winders called swifts.

However, many whalers made scrimshaw which was used aboard ship. Sail makers decorated bone yardsticks, needle cases, and seam rubbers which were used to rub wax into seams in an attempt to preserve them. Coopers carved designs on the bone dipsticks which they used to measure the level of oil in the casks. The crew played with scrimshaw cribbage boards and chess sets they had designed.

Captain Eldredge and Duvall used stamps with decorated handles to stamp into the log book pictures of whales caught or lost. A picture of a full whale meant that the creature had been caught and tried out. A picture of a whale's flukes rising out of the water meant that the whale had escaped.

In the 1800s, every whaling family owned scrimshaw art. Today, many pieces can be seen in museums.

One day the lookout sighted another whaling ship six miles off the larboard bow.

"Square your yards and make for that ship," Captain Eldredge ordered. It was time for a gam, the whaler's term for a party at sea. A gam could last a few hours or a week.

When the ships were less than one mile apart, the Captain of the other ship, his wife who was traveling with him, and a crew were lowered into a whaleboat. The whaleboat crew was needed in case a whale was sighted on the trip to the *Monmouth,* or while the Captain and his wife were visiting on board.

The Captain's wife, in the barrel-like gamming chair, being welcomed aboard.

As the whaleboat reached the *Monmouth,* the gamming chair was lowered for the Captain's wife. The chair looked something like a barrel with one side cut away and a seat added inside. Once the Captain and his wife were on board, Duvall and his whaleboat crew rowed to gam on the other ship. The rest of the crew prepared for the gam, half of the men visiting on the other ship and half remaining on the *Monmouth.*

Such an occasion called for a special meal. So

Whitehouse cooked a lunch of lobscouse and plum duff for all.

Watching for whales never ceased, however. If a whale was sighted during a gam, both ships sent men to catch it. The first boat to harpoon the creature claimed it as its own. The other boats remained a short distance away, ready to help if they were needed.

The crew of both ships were excited. They met new people, sent and received letters, exchanged food and supplies, and heard new jokes and stories about the sea.

Peter met a Portugese boy named Leal de Roza, and heard how he became a crewman on the New Bedford whaler.

"I lived in the Azores Islands off the coast of Portugal, but I wanted to go to America," Leal told Peter. "One day this ship sailed close to our island. A landing party came into the harbor and many of the men ran to the hills to hide with the farmers there. I knew the Captain would need new men, so I slipped into the water and swam out to the ship. It had just left New Bedford, and so I will have to sail with her for two or three years, but finally I will go to America." Peter had to listen very hard. Leal was just learning to speak English and had a very strong accent.

"You know," Peter said to Leal, "I was mighty surprised to see your Captain's wife on board."

"It's not every ship that's a hen frigate, has a woman on board," Leal said. "Some say its bad luck to have a woman, but others say it's better to have one. She keeps the Captain in line, she does, and there's not as much cussin' and swearin' when she's about. We also get punished less for doing wrong.''

The first woman to sail on a whaling ship was Mrs. Mary Russell. After long, lonely months waiting for her husband, Captain Joseph Russell, and her son, William, to return from the sea, she decided she would wait no longer. Taking her youngest son, Charles, with her, she met her husband's ship *Emily* in London, England. From there she had sailed with the ship for the remainder of the voyage.

Life aboard ship was not easy for Mrs. Russell. She was crowded into the small cabin she shared with her husband, and tried to keep busy sewing, washing clothes, giving lessons to her young son, reading, and keeping a diary.

Soon other Captain's wives and children sailed on whaling ships. It was not unusual for a young child to be afraid of land after spending three or four years at sea. Pregnant wives were often left with natives, or in hotels or hospitals to have their children. Their husbands returned for them after the whaling season had ended.

After two days, Captain Eldredge and his guests decided the visit was over. The Captain and his wife returned to their ship. Duvall and the others returned to the *Monmouth*.

7 *Search and Failure*

THE *MONMOUTH* HAD OTHER OPPORTUNITIES FOR A WHALE CHASE. One day, a strong wind blew in the direction of a large sperm whale off the starboard bow.

"Get the sail, boys. Nature herself will see to this one," Captain Eldredge ordered as he settled in the stern of his whaleboat.

The heavy mast pole was secured just behind the bow, and the sail was attached. It filled with wind.

The whale heard the noise of the mast slipping into place, and ran to save its life. For several miles, it swam close to the surface, then sounded out of sight.

Within minutes, it breached above the sea, the silvery water falling from its back. Then like a mountain, the sperm whale came thundering back into the water and dove deep again. The water rose into a violent curtain, and fell into the ocean as the whale disappeared. It surfaced a few miles away. Hours passed. The whale swam on, neither stopping nor slowing its pace to rest.

When the light began to fade and darkness closed in around the whaleboat, Captain Eldredge realized the cause was lost. He ordered the sail to be pulled down, and the boat lay drifting in the calm, dark sea.

The lantern keg, the ship's survival kit, was opened. It contained everything they needed to pass the warm, still night. Captain Eldredge filled the lantern with whale oil, and lit it with matches he found at the bottom of the keg. He gave each

Captain Eldredge points out the stars in the southern sky.

man a ration of hardtack, water, and a plug of tobacco to chew after the meal.

Peter noticed that the southern sky was filled with many more stars than the northern sky over Cold Spring Harbor. Captain Eldredge pointed out the belt of the constellation Orion, "the hunter," and the Southern Cross. These two star groups were used for navigating in the southern hemisphere.

The whalemen tried to rest their tired bodies, but it wasn't easy to sleep in the small, cramped whaleboat. At last, dawn came and they found themselves surrounded by a dense wall of fog. Captain Eldredge thought the *Monmouth* lay to the north, and used his compass to guide them in that direction. By mid morning the rising sun burned off the fog, and the men saw their ship laying before them.

Later that afternoon, the cry from the hoops was heard again: "Thar she blows! A-a-a-ah blows!" Again the crew ran to their whaleboats. This time it was Duvall's men that captured the whale.

It was a baleen whale. Instead of teeth, it had a baleen, over 200 pieces of flexible whalebone hanging from its upper jaw. These strips grew close together, leaving a small space between them. Thousands of tiny fringes lined the inside of the bone. To eat, the whale filled its mouth with great gulps of water, then used its giant tongue to push the water through the baleen which acted as a sieve. The fringes held onto tiny marine organisms so they could not escape with the rushing water.

Baleen whales gave a poorer grade oil than sperm whales. Nevertheless, they were tried out, but their oil was kept separate from the sperm oil.

Healthy looking baleen whales were caught, only to discover they had a dry skin. As a result, there was not enough oil to try out. Others were lost because many species of baleen whales do not float when dead. They sank before the men could bring them alongside the ships.

As the *Monmouth* cruised off the coast of Australia, she sometimes came close to shore looking for provisions. Peter found himself either on harsh desert coastal lands, or on beautiful white sandy beaches. Once, in an area where the plantlife was sparse, he saw some odd looking animals. They stood as tall as himself and moved by taking giant leaps with their hind legs. They carried their young in pouches on their stomachs. Another time he saw a thick, lush eucalyptus forest where teddy bear like creatures watched with curious eyes. The ship sailed along the northeastern coast off the Great Barrier Reef until they put in the harbor at Sydney.

Captain Eldredge gave orders to repair and refit the ship. It was leaking badly.

The whalers looked like a sorry lot as they went ashore. Their clothes had been mended with patches of every shape, color and size. Their skin was red and tough from hard work and weather, and many had beards or clumsily shaved faces.

Some men went directly to the bars and entertainment halls. Others went to the churches to pray. They enjoyed their weeks of liberty in Sydney, but they had little money to spend. Captain Eldredge thought the men would run off if he gave them any money.

When the ship was ready, the crew returned and the *Monmouth* sailed out of the harbor, through Bass Strait between Australia and Tasmania, then westward into the Indian Ocean once more.

8 Storms, Scurvy, and a Refusal to Obey

AS THEY CONTINUED THEIR VOYAGE, WHALES WERE CAUGHT AND lost. The *Monmouth* had been at sea two and one-half years. The fresh food had been eaten long ago. All that remained was dried beef, beans, hardtack biscuits, grain, coffee, tea and molasses. By December, some of the crew became sick with scurvy, a disease caused by the lack of vitamin C in the diet. Captain Eldredge called the crew together and said, "Set your course for land boys, we're bound for Africa."

But the voyage west was full of danger. Storms continually battered the ship. Swelling seas splashed over the decks, flooding the cabins and washing equipment overboard. Howling winds tore at the rigging, ripping the sails, and they had to

The ship is battered by storms.

be repaired. It was a frightening and dangerous situation, but a man was sent aloft. He inched along the slippery deck and clung to the railing as the ship heaved in the storm. Then he climbed up into the rigging and repaired the sails. Whalemen were often killed when fierce winds blew them off the rigging, and they fell onto the deck or disappeared into the sea.

The *Monmouth* fought through the storm, and she began to leak even more than usual. It was impossible to get to the coast of South Africa. They had to set a new course past Africa and into the Atlantic Ocean. They finally sailed toward St. Helena Island.

Before they reached their destination, another whale was sighted. Again the familiar cry came: "Thar she blows!"

Nat Scudder threw the harpoon, and the whale leaped forward in a wild "Nantucket Sleigh Ride." In its frenzy to

The whaleboat is dragged in a "Nantucket Sleigh Ride."

escape, the whale dragged the boat through a line of breakers. The small whaleboat hit the churning water and broke into a thousand pieces. The men and the splintered wood were thrown into the air, then dropped with a splash into the sea to disappear from sight. Captain Eldredge searched for the men, but all he found were the remains of the boat.

Several days later, St. Helena Island was sighted. The ship, filled with sick crewmen and a leaking hull, limped into Jamestown Harbor, the island's main port. Captain Eldredge did not have to pay the men who were sick. The Whaleman's Shipping Articles stated that any man who left the ship before the end of the voyage would give up his lay. But the Captain refused to leave his men penniless. He gave each man three months pay, then sent them to the hospital.

While the *Monmouth* was in the harbor, the whaling ship *Hannah Brewer,* moored nearby, was declared dangerous and unfit to continue sailing. She had 115 casks of oil on board. Captain Eldredge wanted to take this oil on board as freight. He ordered his crewmen to transfer the casks to his ship, but they refused. They said the articles did not include transferring oil from one ship to another. They were also afraid the added weight would cause the ship to leak even more. Captain Eldredge persuaded the men to go with him to the local shipping agent's office. Neither the agent nor the Captain could convince the crew to do the work.

The men were taking a chance in refusing to obey orders.

Most Captains would not have allowed such behavior. Discipline on most ships was strict. Men who dared to disobey were punished as mutineers.

On the New Bedford ship *Condor,* the Captain whipped men for his own amusement. Daniel Weston Hall was fifteen years old when he signed on the *Condor.* The year was 1856. The *Monmouth* was still at sea.

Daniel and a friend were wrestling in the forecastle. There was nothing wrong in this; the men often held friendly wrestling matches when they had no work to do. On this particular day, the Captain was in a bad mood. He ordered the boys to fight on deck so that everyone could see them. The loser would be beaten with the whip. The boys knew they could not refuse. If they did, they would be punished.

The boys tried to put on a good show, but the Captain was not satisfied. He ordered Daniel to take his shirt off and hold onto the side of the ship. The Captain gave Daniel 18 lashes with the whip. Then he whipped Daniel's friend and told him to give Daniel six more lashes. At last the beating ended for Daniel. As he was being led to his bunk, his friend was being whipped once again by the Captain.

Through all of this, the crew stood by and watched. They did not dare to interfere. The Captain was the supreme commander. They knew that if they tried to help the boys, they would have been whipped, too.

Perhaps the men of the *Monmouth* planned to run away if

the Captain tried to punish them. Or perhaps they hoped he would not punish them once they were at sea. Perhaps they knew the Captain was a fair man and would not punish them at all. We do not know. But in the end, Captain Eldredge had to pay the crew of the *Hannah Brewer* to transfer the oil.

Soon it was time for Captain Eldredge to set a course for home. Several men were hired to take the place of those still in the hospital, and the *Monmouth* sailed out of the harbor. The voyage home was uneventful. On June 6, 1857, the ship lowered the anchor off the sandbar in Cold Spring Harbor. She had logged 30 months at sea.

Friends and relatives crowded the wharf and greeted the tired, homesick whalers. Stevedores unloaded the oil and equipment. The oil went to the warehouses to be stored and later sold. Sperm oil was sent to the refinery to be divided into oil and spermaceti. Finally, the men returned to John Jones' general store to receive their lays.

Most whalers received very little for their work. In 1841, the ship *Elizabeth* returned home after three years and five months at sea. One man, John Oliver, received $5.39 for his share of the profits. Since whalers had to pay for the outfits they received before each voyage, and for any items they bought from the slop chest, many men found themselves in debt to the company. They had to sign on another voyage in order to try to pay their debt. We have no records to show how much money Peter Dumont collected for his share of the profits, but we can assume the amount was small.

At first Peter thought he would never return to a whaling ship, but the whaler's life, though full of danger, accidents and even death, also had the attraction of adventure, of visiting strange countries and seeing new sights. And there was also the intense excitement of the hunts themselves. Peter talked with other greenhands of whaling in the Arctic, and seeing snow white polar bears and the giant ice floes. He once wrote, "A whaler, with a pipe in his mouth, is ready to meet anything on earth, be it whale or whirlwind."

9 *The Death of American Whaling*

THE CREWMEN OF COLD SPRING HARBOR WERE NOT THE ONLY men returning to whaling ships. The ports of New England were thriving, and in 1857 New Bedford had its most successful year with a fleet of 329 whaling ships. But as time went on, more and more whales were taken from the sea, and soon they became fewer in number and harder to find.

A young man named Herman Melville joined the crew of a whaling ship, and saw this happening. Several years later, he wrote *Moby Dick*. In this book he warned that if too many whales were captured, they would soon disappear from the seas. Melville had good cause to worry. In the 12th century A.D., the Basques, a people living near the Bay of Biscay in

Spain, hunted the Biscay right whales until they killed almost every one of them.

As whales grew scarce, voyages became longer, more men were needed for each voyage, and ships returned home with less oil each year. Investors began putting their money into other industries. The whalers themselves were leaving the ships to work in the newly developing textile industry.

Gold was discovered in California. Hundreds of men and officers left their ships at sea or in the California harbors. They went to the gold fields to try to get rich quick. Other officers joined the merchant ships or whaling fleets of other countries.

During the Civil War, the Confederate army did not want ships carrying valuable cargo to reach northern ports. Many whaling ships returning home, not knowing about the war, were captured and sometimes destroyed by Confederate warships, such as the *Shenandoah*.

American whaling was dying, and an incident in 1871 hurried it along. The Eskimos in the Artic warned of an early winter, but whaling captains refused to believe them. That winter 33 ships were crushed in the Arctic ice. Over the next 23 years, more than 39 ships were lost in storms or abandoned.

The end of whaling by American ships was made certain in 1859, when petroleum was discovered in Pennsylvania. People began using kerosene instead of whale oil. By 1920, only two large whaling ships were still sailing out of the United States. One of these, the *Wanderer*, was wrecked off the coast of Massachusetts. The other ship, the *Charles W. Morgan,* can still be seen at the whaling museum called The Mystic Seaport, Mystic, Connecticut.

Whaling would have died all around the world had it not been for two inventions. The first was the harpoon gun invented by a Norwegian named Svend Foyn. The second was the use of the steamship. By mounting the harpoon gun onto

During the winter of 1871, 33 ships were crushed in the Arctic ice.

the steamship, whales could be hunted faster and more efficiently. Whaling around the world increased.

The old whalers hunted right and sperm whales because they were slow, and they floated when dead. Today, the whalers inject compressed air into the carcasses which causes them to float. The combination of speed and modern equipment means that no species is too fast or too clever to escape.

During the last fifty years, hunters using this modern equipment have killed over two million whales. Most whales have disappeared from northern waters, and a number of species are now on the endangered list. But two countries—Japan and the Soviet Union—continue to hunt. They know that whales go to feed in southern waters during the Antarctic summer. Modern ships leave Japan and the Soviet Union at the end of October, and arrive at the whaling grounds when the whales reach the area in early January.

Instead of six-man whaleboats, catcher boats carrying eleven men and a harpooner, are used. Helicopters leave the deck of the ship and locate the whales for the catcher boats. If the whale dives, it is picked up on sonar equipment and followed. When it surfaces, the boat races into position, and harpoons the whale. Modern harpoons do not simply catch the whale, they kill it. Usually one explosive harpoon is enough, although sometimes two are used.

Today's ships are specially built floating factories. They have crews of 500 or more men and women. The whales are

A cut-away view of a modern factory ship.

1. Slipway
2. Hospital
3. Recreation room
4. Crew's quarters
5. Flensing deck
6. Lemming deck
7. Factory area
8. Navigating bridge and officers' quarters
9. Radio room
10. Crew's quarters and mess area
11. Refrigeration plant
12. Stores and provisions

hauled on board through a ramp, onto the flensing deck. There they are cut up and sent to various parts of the ship. The meat goes to the freezers. The blubber goes to the mincing machines, then to steam cookers where it is melted into oil. The head and bones go to power saws, then to special cookers to have their oil extracted. On some ships, the liver is sent to the liver extraction plant, and other parts are sent to chemical labs. The entire process takes less than one hour. Some ships can take on as many as twenty-four whales in one day.

In an attempt to help whales, the International Whaling Commission meets every year in London, England. They talk about the best ways to help the whales survive. They set quotas on how many whales each country may kill. In recent years, the quota has been reduced, because some kinds of whales are getting more and more scarce. But the quotas are voluntary. There is no way to force countries to accept or obey the limits, and poaching and breaking of agreements are common.

Female whales swimming with young calves are supposed to be avoided, but modern whalers kill the calves in order to attract and catch the parents. Young whales are also protected by international law, but whalers often kill any whale they can find. The 1978 endangered species list of animals that are now very rare includes eight species of whales, and *all* the whales mentioned in this book.

The United States is leading the fight to save the whales.

In 1972, Congress passed the Marine Mammal Protection Act, which prevents American citizens from harming, bothering or killing marine mammals anywhere in the world. It also prohibits Americans from catching whales unless they have permission from a special scientific committee.

The United States government wants all whaling to stop for ten years, in the hope that this period will give the whales time to have enough offspring to regain their once great numbers. But Japan and the Soviet Union, which do 85% of today's whaling, do not believe this is necessary. They say that if all the countries follow the quotas, the whales will be protected.

No one really knows what effect limited whaling will have on the future of the animals. Scientists have found out some things about sea mammals. They know whales live in families. Killer whales have been known to stay in the same family for periods of up to ten years and longer.

Whales are good, loving parents. They will sacrifice themselves in order to save their mate or their young, and they feel grief when a member of the family dies. A baby whale was accidentally killed by the propeller of a ship. The mother took her baby in her mouth. Hour after hour, day after day, she brought it to the surface to make it breath. Weeks later, another ship reported seeing the mother still bringing the dead baby up to the surface.

Products taken from the whale continue to be in demand

Day after day, the mother whale brought her dead baby to the surface, trying to make it breathe.

around the world. Whale meat is eaten in Greenland, Iceland, Japan and parts of Europe. The humpback whale gives a poor grade of oil, but it can give up to 80,000 pounds of meat. That is equal to 133 head of cattle.

Japan claims that it does not have enough room to raise cattle. That is why they depend on whale meat, which is served in their homes, schools and restaurants.

Vitamins A and B are extracted from the whale's liver. Its oil is used in steel, paints, varnishes, linoleum, water proofing products, candles, woolens, face creams, and pet food. Whale meal is used to feed cattle.

Despite this, is whaling still necessary? Petroleum, natural gas and electricity have replaced the need for oil and spermaceti candles. Modern medicines are used in place of whale oil ointments. Vitamins and other chemicals can be found in other sources or made synthetically. Scientists have found a way to reproduce ambergris, and fats and other foods can be used in face creams. Metals and plastics have replaced the need for whalebone in everything from springs to fine surgical instruments.

Scientists at the National Academy of Science in Washington D.C. have discovered a substitute for sperm oil. They have found that the *jojoba* (pronounced ho-ho-bah) bean gives an oil that is of a higher quality than sperm oil for today's uses. The bean grows wild in parts of California, Arizona, and Mexico. Dr. Noel Vietmeyer of the Academy and others have started to grow the beans on plantations. If jojoba beans can be produced cheaply, they may become more popular than sperm oil. That could mean the end of the whale oil business. As Dr. Vietmeyer once said, "That's a lot of lives in exchange for a crop of beans."

Index